OFF TO MAHARASHTRA

SONIA MEHTA

PUFFIN BOOKS

PUFFIN BOOKS

USA | Canada | UK | Ireland | Australia | New Zealand | India | South Africa | China

Puffin Books is part of the Penguin Random House group of companies whose addresses can be found at global.penguinrandomhouse.com

Published by Penguin Random House India Pvt. Ltd
7th Floor, Infinity Tower C, DLF Cyber City,
Gurgaon 122 002, Haryana, India

First published in Puffin Books by Penguin Random House India 2017

Text, design and illustrations copyright © Quadrum Solutions Pvt. Ltd 2017
Series copyright © Penguin Random House India 2017

Picture Credits

P 8: Matheran (© Nicholas (Nichalp) (Own work, touched up in Photoshop) [CC BY-SA 2.5 (http://creativecommons.org/licenses/by-sa/2.5)], via Wikimedia Commons); P 11: Cerebrum IT Park, Pune (© Conceptorm [CC BY-SA 3.0 (http://creativecommons.org/licenses/by-sa/3.0)], via Wikimedia Commons), Grape vineyards, Nashik (© Pablo Ares Gastesi (Flickr: pb010032) [CC BY-SA 2.0 (http://creativecommons.org/licenses/by-sa/2.0)], via Wikimedia Commons); P 13: Pride of India (© Lokenrc [CC BY 2.5 (http://creativecommons.org/licenses/by/2.5)], via Wikimedia Commons), Indian giant squirrel (© Yathin S Krishnappa (Own work) [CC BY-SA 3.0 (http://creativecommons.org/licenses/by-sa/3.0)], via Wikimedia Commons), Yellow-footed green pigeon (© Harvinder Chandigarh (Own work) [CC BY-SA 4.0 (http://creativecommons.org/licenses/by-sa/4.0)], via Wikimedia Commons); P 14: Xuanzang (© Charlie (Own work) [CC BY-SA 4.0 (http://creativecommons.org/licenses/by-sa/4.0)], via Wikimedia Commons); P 18: Balaji Vishwanath (© Amit20081980 (Own work) [CC BY-SA 4.0 (http://creativecommons.org/licenses/by-sa/4.0)], via Wikimedia Commons); P 28: Ganpati immersion (CRS PHOTO/Shutterstock.com); P 32: Pratapgad (© Yogesh Ponkshe); P 33: Raigad fort (© Swapnaannjames [GFDL (http://www.gnu.org/copyleft/fdl.html) or CC-BY-SA-3.0 (http://creativecommons.org/licenses/by-sa/3.0/)], via Wikimedia Commons); P 42: Paithani weavers (© Orapin Joyphuem/Shutterstock.com), Kolhapuri shoe makers (© clicksabhi/Shutterstock.com)

All rights reserved

10 9 8 7 6 5 4 3 2 1

The views and opinions expressed in this book are the author's own and the facts are as reported by her, which have been verified to the extent possible, and the publishers are not in any way liable for the same.

The information in this book is based on research from bonafide sites and published books and is true to the best of the author's knowledge at the time of going to print. The author is not responsible for any further changes or developments occurring post the publication of this book. This series is not a comprehensive representation of the states of India but is intended to give children a flavour of the lifestyles and cultures of different states. All illustrations are artistic representations only.

ISBN 9780143440789

Design and layout by Quadrum Solutions Pvt. Ltd
Printed at Replika Press Pvt. Ltd, India

This book is sold subject to the condition that it shall not, by way of trade or otherwise, be lent, resold, hired out, or otherwise circulated without the publisher's prior consent in any form of binding or cover other than that in which it is published and without a similar condition including this condition being imposed on the subsequent purchaser.

www.penguin.co.in

Hello Kids!

I'm so happy you are reading this book. India is an incredible country and there are lots of things about it that we never get to hear about.

I discovered India because my father was in the Indian army. He was posted to many places all over India—and we dutifully followed him. Can you imagine that by the time I was in the tenth standard, I had changed nine schools? Of course it was hard making new friends almost every year, but the good part was that I got to live in so many places. Right from Kerala, where I was born, to Kashmir, Jhansi, Shillong, Chandigarh, Goa . . . the list is long.

Every time I go to a new place, I feel amazed at how different each state is from the other—and yet, how similar. Did you know that we can see monuments from the Stone Age right here in India? Or that we have more than twenty official languages, and most Indians know three or four on an average? Or even that some of the world's most amazing scientific marvels were invented in India?

Oh, there are many, many, many fun and fantastic things about the states of India, which we simply must get to know.

So get your backpack ready, get set to meet some new friends and join me on a fun trip as we **DISCOVER INDIA, STATE BY STATE.**

I hope you enjoy reading this book as much as I have enjoyed writing it. I would love to hear from you. So do write to me at sonia.mehta@quadrumltd.com.

Lots of love,
Sonia Aunty

Mishki and Pushka have come to visit Earth from their home planet, Zoomba. They have never seen such an amazing place. Zoomba doesn't have trees and mountains and rivers like Earth does. But the people look exactly the same. When they come to Earth, they meet a sweet old man whom they call Daadu Dolma. Daadu Dolma shows them all the wonderful places in India and tells Mishki and Pushka all about them.

Mishki and Pushka can't believe what they see. They have seen a lot of Earth, but they have never, ever seen a place like India.

They are off to explore India state by state :)

Mishki

Mishki is a curious little girl. She is always asking loads of questions. On her home planet, she is always getting into trouble for poking her nose into things that are not her business.

Pushka

Pushka is Mishki's brother. He *loves adventure*. He is always ready to try a new challenge. Whether it's climbing a mountain, or diving into a cold, cold sea, he is up for it.

Daadu Dolma

Daadu Dolma is a wise old man who has lived on Earth longer than the mountains and seas. No one knows quite how old he is, but he certainly has been around. He knows everything about everything.

Mishki and Pushka simply can't be still. They are going to visit a state they have heard so much about.

'I've heard that Maharashtra has an amazing history,' says Mishki.

'I just want to try the food,' says Pushka.

'Oh, you're so boring. You're always hungry,' Mishki says impatiently.

'Well, then,' says Daadu Dolma, laughing. 'You are not going to be disappointed. Because you are both right. You will find Maharashtra amazing.'

'So shall we just go?' asks Pushka jumping up and down.

'Yes, let's go,' says Daadu Dolma. 'Come and hold on tight.'

Mishki and Pushka clap their hands in delight. They are

OFF TO MAHARASHTRA!!!

Land ahoy!

"Daadu Dolma, does the word 'Maharashtra' mean anything?"

"Yes. 'Maha' means great. 'Rashtra' actually means nation, but here it refers to a state. So 'Maharashtra' means great state."

Maharashtra is the third largest state in India. So it really is a great state!

FRIENDLY NEIGHBOURS

This state has many neighbours. There's Gujarat to the north-west, Madhya Pradesh to the north, Chhattisgarh to the east, Telangana to the south-east, Karnataka to the south and Goa to the south-west. To its west is the vast and wonderful Arabian Sea. No wonder Maharashtra has so many coastal cities!

ON THE MAP

To see exactly where Maharashtra is on the map of India, go to http://www.mapsofindia.com/maps/india/india-political-map.htm

JUST LIKE A BACKBONE

Just like all of us have a backbone, Maharashtra has a backbone too! And that is the Sahyadri mountain range, which is a part of the Western Ghats. This mountain range slices right through the middle of Maharashtra and has a lot of the state's history hidden in its forests.

HILLS AND VALLEYS AND HILLS

The Western Ghats are a series of mountains, hills and valleys with narrow roads cutting through them. It is perfect for guerrilla warfare, which Shivaji Maharaj, the famous Maratha king, was renowned for. Several Maratha forts dot these hills. To the north run the Satpura Hills. They are shared by Gujarat.

COASTING ALONG

Between the Arabian Sea and the Sahyadris is a long, luscious strip of land called the Konkan Coast. It is famous not just for its beauty but also for its yummy food!

FLAT LIKE A TABLE

A lot of Maharashtra is a plateau—what we also call a tableland because it is flat like a table. This region is called the Deccan Plateau. It is enormous and covers many other states as well.

How cool! I would love to explore the Deccan Traps.

Did you know?
The Deccan Plateau runs across the states of Telangana, Andhra Pradesh, Karnataka, Kerala and parts of Tamil Nadu and Goa too!

TRAPPED BY LAVA

Imagine enormous volcanoes spewing out tonnes of lava. Now imagine the lava hardening over centuries and creating many, many ridges and hollows. That is what has happened in the Deccan region. These hollows and ridges are called the Deccan Traps.

Oh Wow!
Hundreds of volcanoes erupted over sixty million years ago in this region and created the Deccan Traps.

HOTSPOT FORESTS

Guess what! The forests in the Western Ghats are believed to be among the world's eight 'hottest hotspots' because of the kind of plant and animal life they have. There are more than 300 types of animals, birds, reptiles and plants here. Some are so rare that they are on the watch list for extinction.

The Asian elephant, tiger, gaur, lion-tailed macaque, Nilgiri tahr and Nilgiri langur are some of the endangered creatures that live in the Western Ghats.

SIX PACK

Maharashtra is basically divided into six regions. You must have heard of many of these and maybe even live in one of them.

- AMRAVATI
- AURANGABAD (also called Marathwada)
- KONKAN (of which the famous Mumbai city is a part)
- NAGPUR
- NASHIK
- PUNE

WHAT'S ODD?

Pushka sees something odd in each row. Can you circle the one that is odd?

| GUJARAT | MADHYA PRADESH | MAHARASHTRA | ARABIAN SEA |

| SAHYADRI | LAKE MICHIGAN | SATPURA | HIMALAYAS |

| HILLS | VALLEYS | MALLS | RIVERS |

CITY CITY BANG BANG

Maharashtra has some of India's largest and busiest cities. Let's explore some of them.

SUPER BUSY MUMBAI

Mumbai (it used to be called Bombay) is a super busy, super crowded city. People compare it to New York because it has the same hustle and bustle. It is also the capital of Maharashtra. And the finance capital of India too.

Queen's Necklace

THE HISTORY OF MUMBAI

Did you know that Mumbai is actually made of seven islands? It is believed that these seven islands were once a part of King Ashoka's kingdom. Many hundreds of years later, the Portuguese seized these islands and controlled trade from here. The islands were the dowry of a Portuguese princess named Catherine de Braganza when she married King Charles II of England. Later, he gave them to the East India Company when the British took over India. Gosh, quite a history!

PUNE: ANCIENT AND MODERN

This city is a perfect example of 'new India'. It has a tremendous history too because King Shivaji lived here for a while. Now it has factories, industries and IT parks, and it's super modern and super cool!

NASHIK: THE GRAPE CITY

Nashik is a city that is so old that its residents claim that Ram and Sita lived here during their exile. The legend goes that this is where Ram and his brother Laxman cut off the nose of the evil princess Surpanakha and threw it across the river. Nashik, in fact, means nose. Today, Nashik is a modern city with lots of industries. It is also famous for its grape vineyards where wine is made.

Finger Painting

Mishki has gone grape picking in Nashik. Her fingers have become sticky and purple. She has made a bunch of grapes using her fingerprints. Can you do it too? Simply dip your fingers in purple paint, and then press them on a sheet of paper like she did. Then draw the leaves and voila! Your finger grapes are ready!

Paint here

RAIN, RAIN, DON'T GO AWAY!

Just like most of India, Maharashtra has a hot, tropical climate. The summers are scorching. The rains in June bring with them a rich green cover, and for a while everyone celebrates this wonderful weather. Then, the nasty October heat makes everything dusty and brown. Finally, a gentle winter arrives to soothe everyone.
The Konkan Coast faces the fury of the monsoon when it's at its peak.

CROP HOP

With so many rivers and such a rich land, farming is very important in Maharashtra. Many different crops are grown here, like wheat, rice, jowar, pulses and bajra. But there are also yummy fruits—oranges in Nagpur, grapes in Nashik and mangoes along the Konkan strip. And sugar cane! Maharashtra grows lots of sugar cane. Groundnut, cotton and tobacco are other 'cash crops'.

ROARING RIVERS

Many rivers are born in the Western Ghats. Some of these, along with their tributaries, flow into the east, looking for the Bay of Bengal. The main ones are the Godavari and the Krishna. There are some that rush towards the Arabian Sea on the west. These are the Tapi and the Narmada. Thanks to these rivers, most of Maharashtra is rich and fertile.

FUN FACTS

State Flower — Pride of India

State animal — Indian giant squirrel

State bird — Yellow-footed green pigeon

State tree — Mango

CRAZY CROSSWORD

Pushka and Mishki want to make sure they remember everything they have learnt. Help them fill in this crossword so they don't forget.

Across
2. A crop beginning with 'B' that is grown in Maharashtra
5. A famous river that ends in A
7. A region in Maharashtra that has 4 letters
8. A soft, white cash crop grown in Maharashtra
10. Tangy fruits that are grown in Nagpur.
12. Tobacco, cotton and sugar cane are all called ____ crops
13. Maharashtra is hot and humid because it is in the _____
14. When land is rich and good for growing crops, this is what it is called

Down
1. Another word for seasonal rain
3. A crop beginning with 'R' that is grown in Maharashtra
4. The yummy fruit that grows in the Konkan region
6. A rainy month
9. A river that rushes down from the hills
11. The fox found them sour, but people in Maharashtra love them

Long, long ago

Daadu, what is different about Maharashtra's history?

Well, one amazing fact is that one of Maharashtra's great kings, Shivaji Maharaj, has a huge following in Maharashtra to this day! Very few kings have this kind of following.

MANY SMALL KINGDOMS

The first time Maharashtra was written about was in the seventh century. A Chinese traveller called Xuanzang wrote about this land. In those days, the region was made up of many smaller Hindu kingdoms. These were the Satavahanas, the Vakatakas, the Kalachuris, the Rashtrakutas, the Chalukyas and the Yadavas.

Xuanzang, the Chinese traveller

ATTACK!!!

With so many small kingdoms, it was easy for any other strong army to attack. The Muslim rulers saw an opportunity and defeated these kingdoms. They ruled for many years, but soon they began to fight amongst themselves. There was chaos. It was the perfect time for a new leader to arrive on the scene. And he did.

A MAN NAMED SHIVAJI

Muslim rule was all over India. The Mughals were in the north, and Sultans of Bijapur were in the south. They ruled their kingdom with an iron hand. This made a young sixteen-year-old very angry. He decided he had to do something about this terrible situation. That youth's name was Shivaji.

Shivaji was so smart that he collected a band of followers that grew into an army. Over the next several years, he built a vast Maratha empire and challenged the Mughals.

THE STORY OF SHIVAJI MAHARAJ

Shivaji was born in a place called Shivneri in Pune. His ancestors were noblemen but not kings. Shivaji was not only very clever and daring but also a military genius. He came up with clever plans to fool and overpower his enemies. His first conquest was when he captured the fort of Torna. Soon, he began to capture fort after fort after fort, threatening the Mughals in the north and the Sultans in the south.

Shivaji was called the Mountain Rat because he was so nimble that he could scurry in and out of the mountains like a rat.

THE SULTAN'S REPLY

When the Sultan of Bijapur heard of Shivaji's conquests, he sent a strong army of nearly 20,000 soldiers, led by a warrior called Afzal Khan, to capture and kill Shivaji. But Shivaji was too clever. He lured Afzal Khan's army deep into the forests of the Western Ghats that he knew so well, which the Muslim troops got lost in. He not only killed Afzal Khan but also took control of the troops, the army horses, the guns and all the ammunition. Imagine how strong that made Shivaji!

A DRAMATIC ESCAPE

Aurangzeb

The Mughal emperor Aurangzeb was now worried about Shivaji. He came up with a plan of his own. He invited Shivaji to Agra (which was the Mughal capital at that time) to discuss peace. When Shivaji came along with his son Sambhaji, he arrested them both. But Shivaji was much too clever. He and his son hid in two baskets of fruit that were being sent out of the city. That's how Shivaji escaped from right under the noses of the guards who were supposed to watch him. Shivaji was welcomed home with much celebration. Finally, he became the official king. He was now on known as Chhatrapati Shivaji Maharaj.

NO STOPPING SHIVAJI MAHARAJ

There was no stopping Shivaji. His people adored him. He was a good king and believed that people of all religions must live together happily. He built a navy, like the British. He believed in justice at all costs. Under him, the Maratha Empire flourished, and people were happy and prosperous. He died of an illness in Raigad, a mountain fort.

Did you know?
Shivaji's sword was called Bhavani. The story goes that Goddess Bhavani appeared and gave it to Shivaji when he was about to go to war.

LIFE AFTER SHIVAJI

After Shivaji died, his son Sambhaji became king. But he was not as good as his father and was not able to manage the kingdom. Slowly, the Peshwas started gaining control.

Balaji Vishwanath

THE PESHWAS

The Peshwas were basically like prime ministers to the Maratha kings. But with a weak king, they took more and more control of matters. And thus began the decline of the Maratha Empire. The Peshwas became virtual kings and began to take all decisions.

SOME OF THE PESHWAS

Balaji Vishwanath

Baji Rao I

Balaji Baji Rao (Nana Saheb Peshwa)

Madhav Rao I

Narayan Rao

Raghunath Rao (Raghoba Dada)

Madhav Rao II

Baji Rao II

CHIEFS AND CHIEFTAINS

All this while, in the heart of Maharashtra, there were smaller chiefs who were ruling over their own little territories. Gaikwads, Scindias and Holkars were some of these. The British were already making their presence felt along the western coast. Then one day, the British took control of the island of Bombay. And soon, all of India was under the British.

A Scindia Maharaja

Yashwantrao Holkar I

A Gaikwad Ruler

THE BRITISH SPREAD

The British captured Ahmednagar Fort, and that was the last straw. They established military rule over the entire Deccan region. The Peshwas remained rulers only for namesake. The British then established what they called the Bombay Presidency. In those days, this also included parts of the present state of Gujarat.

WORD GRID

There are names of six historical figures hidden in this grid. Find them all!

D	E	P	S	H	I	V	A	J	I	D
B	F	E	E	F	G	R	J	V	E	A
A	F	S	A	M	B	H	A	J	I	C
J	C	H	C	W	B	W	E	F	B	D
I	C	W	V	S	D	S	S	F	H	G
R	C	A	F	Z	A	L	K	H	A	N
A	U	R	A	N	G	Z	E	B	B	V
O	V	B	U	E	F	X	W	V	F	E

FIGHT FOR INDEPENDENCE

Soon, India was completely under British rule. But the people were not happy. They began to fight for independence. All of India now had a common enemy—the British. After many years of struggle and fighting, in 1947 the British finally left India.

First Republic Day parade

BOMBAY STATE

Once the British went away, the leaders of India had to decide what to do next. They put their heads together and decided to name Bombay Presidency 'Bombay State'. The area that was called Baroda (now in Gujarat) was also a part of the state of Bombay.

MAHARASHTRA

GUJARAT

DIVIDED BY LANGUAGE

Gujarati speaking people lived on in Gujarat

It so happened that the people living in the northern part of Bombay State spoke Gujarati, while people in the southern part spoke Marathi. So it was decided that based on the languages, Bombay State would be divided into Maharashtra, where people spoke Marathi, and Gujarat, where people spoke Gujarati.

Marathi speaking people lived on in Maharashtra

A NEW CAPITAL

The city of Bombay, which remained in the Marathi speaking part, became the capital of Maharashtra. Many years later, the name of Bombay changed to Mumbai.

Did you know?

People say the name Mumbai comes from 'Mumba Aai'. Mumba is a goddess that the Mumbai fisherfolk prayed to. Aai means 'mother' in Marathi. That's how the name originated. The British could not pronounce it and called it Bombay instead.

HIDDEN Words

INDEPENDENCE

Such a long word! How many smaller words can you make from it? Mishki made at least ten.

_____ _____ _____ _____

_____ _____ _____ _____

- Come/Go = Yay/Zaa
- Here/There = Ikade/Tikade
- What is your name? = Tumchey nao kaay?
- My name is Pushka = Mazzey nao Pushka aahe
- Thank you! = Dhanyavaad!
- I don't want = Mala nako
- I want = Mala pahije
- Water = Paani
- Where? = Kuthey?
- Let us go = Chala, aapan zaaooya
- I cannot speak Marathi = Mala Marathi yet nahi
- Tomorrow = Udya
- Yesterday = Kaal
- Day after tomorrow = Parva
- What is the time? = Kiti vaazle?
- Come soon = Lavkar yay

MATCH THE WORDS

Don't look at the words you've just learned. Now match the Marathi words to their meanings.

| Where? | Tomorrow | Day after tomorrow | Come soon | Thank you | I don't want |

| Kuthey? | Lavkar yay | Dhanyavaad | Mala nako | Parva | Udya |

A peep into their life

SONGS IN PRAISE OF SHIVAJI

Powada is a style of music wherein the singers praise Shivaji's greatness and bravery. Great poets like Tulsidas and Shahir Agindas wrote these songs, describing the wars and escapades of the great king.

LAVANI

This is an amazing and energetic mix of music and dance. It started as being entertainment for exhausted soldiers. Slowly, it evolved into a proper show in villages. Women and men perform on a makeshift stage. Women wear their sari in a different style that makes it easy for them to move. They sing songs of love. Oh, you can't sit still while a lavani performance is on. You have to clap along.

NATYA SANGEET

People from Maharashtra love plays. Natya Sangeet is a performance where the music is the star of the show. This music is semi-classical in nature.

ABHANG

This is a song that is a prayer to God Vitthal, whom people also call Vithoba. Some really great poets like Dnyandev and Tukaram wrote many abhangas that are sung joyously by people even today.

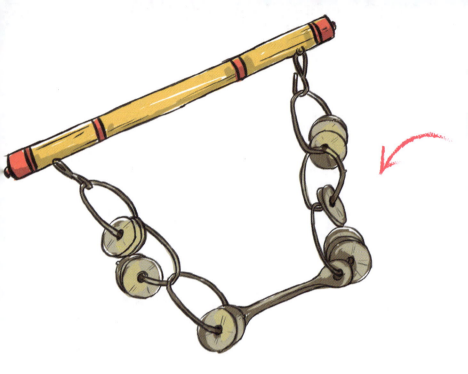

TO THE BEAT OF A STICK

Lezim is an amazing dance in which men dance in rows with lezims in their hand. Lezims are wooden sticks with attached cymbals. The men create their own music by stamping their feet and waving the sticks so that the cymbals create beats.

MAKING MUCH OF BULLS

Maharashtra has many farmers. They have bulls that work hard to plough their fields. Pola is a festival during which farmers appreciate these hard-working animals, without whom their lives would be unimaginable. They bathe their bulls and decorate them. They cook special food that they share with other villagers. And then, they take the bulls through the village, singing and dancing and making much of them.

GREAT POETS

Literature is also very important in Maharashtra. There have been some amazing poets who have written songs and poems that are sung even centuries later. Dnyandev, his sister, Muktabai, and his two brothers were poet saints. Dnyandev wrote a famous book called Dnyaneshwari, in which he wrote about the Bhagwad Gita.

Sant Dnyandev

Sant Eknath

Sant Tukaram

A POETIC TRIO

Three other poet saints, whose names are always taken together, are Eknath, Namdev and Tukaram. They wrote many abhangas and lots of devotional poetry that is sung in temples and homes even today, hundreds of years later.

Sant Namdev

FANTASTIC FESTIVALS

Apart from national festivals like Diwali, Holi, Christmas and Eid, here are some of the other festivals that are celebrated in Maharashtra with great excitement.

GANPATI BAPPA MORYA

During Ganesh Chaturthi, idols of Ganesha are brought home. These idols can be tiny or even as big as a five-story building. After praying to Lord Ganesha for ten days, people take the idols to the sea or the river to immerse them. They make delicious sweets and food during this festival. Lord Ganpati's favourite food, the modak, is especially important. It's great fun!

Did you know?
Ganpati has 108 names! There isn't enough space here to name them all. But you can use the Internet to find them.

OH 'GUDI'!

Gudi Padva marks the Maharashtrian new year. It also marks the beginning of the harvest season. People attach a vessel to the end of a pole and decorate it with flowers and leaves. They then place this on window sills or balconies. This is called the Gudi. People believe it keeps evil out and brings prosperity to the house. Of course, there are sweets and yummy food too!

GOVINDA ALA RE ALA

This amazing festival is celebrated on Janmashtami, which is the day Lord Krishna was born. Lord Krishna loved butter. He would climb on to the shoulders of his friends to get to the butter his mother would hang out of his reach. To celebrate his birth, people hang a mud pot full of goodies as high as two or three storeys of a building. People make a human pyramid, and one brave youth gets to the top and breaks the pot. Then, they all share the goodies.

I would love to try this!

SNAKE SAVIOURS

In some regions, people pray to the cobra (also called 'nag'). They believe that snakes keep their crops safe from pests. On Nag Panchami, they feed milk to snakes and visit Shiva temples, as Lord Shiva always has a snake draped around his shoulders.

SHADOW PLAY

Can you help Mishki match the matki to its shadow?

A   B   C

Bricks and stones

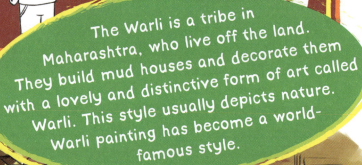

The Warli is a tribe in Maharashtra, who live off the land. They build mud houses and decorate them with a lovely and distinctive form of art called Warli. This style usually depicts nature. Warli painting has become a world-famous style.

V FOR VAADA

A vaada is a traditional home found in many parts of Maharashtra. It is a building with two or more floors, all arranged around a central courtyard. This amazing design first appeared during the Peshwa rule. Usually these vaadas were owned by the rich, like traders or relatives of the Peshwas.

PETH PERFECT

The land around the vaadas was called peth. These were clusters of houses and were quite complete in themselves. Very often, the peths were named after the days of the week. That is why you will find places such as Budhwar (Wednesday) Peth in Pune.

CHAWL

Another style of homes, especially in cities like Mumbai and Pune, is the chawl. These were built mainly for people working in mills. Chawls usually comprise four to five floors. They have large common balconies, which are shared by all the residents. Even the bathrooms are common, and there is great community life here, with people getting together when they fill water, celebrate festivals or just sit around and chat.

WORD LADDER

Can you turn the word CHAWL into ALE? As you go up the ladder, change one letter each time to make the next. Follow the clues given alongside.

A	L	E	
			(Everything)
			(You find it in cricket and in hockey too)
			(To cry loudly)
			(Walking on all fours)
C	H	A	W	L

31

Standing strong

I can see a whole lot of forts here, Daadu. Why is that?

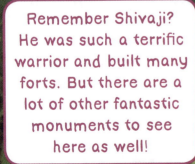

Remember Shivaji? He was such a terrific warrior and built many forts. But there are a lot of other fantastic monuments to see here as well!

PRATAPGAD FORT

This superb fort was built by Shivaji to keep an eye on things from a high mountain near the town of Mahabaleshwar. It was from this fort that he defeated Afzal Khan. And it was supposed to be here that his famous Bhavani sword was given to him by Goddess Bhavani. There is a steep fall from one of the sides. There are rumours that traitors were punished by being pushed off this steep cliff.

THE GIBRALTAR OF THE EAST

The British gave this name to Raigad Fort because it was almost impossible to get past it. This was where Shivaji was crowned king and also where he died. It is high up on a hill and not easy to get to. But once you're there, it has magnificent views you can enjoy—if you don't get blown away by the wind, that is. There were separate quarters for the queen and her ladies, and Shivaji had his own personal palace too.
There was also a separate gateway called Palkhi Darwaja, from where Shivaji would enter along with his convoy.

AHMEDNAGAR FORT

This was built by a sultan called Ahmed Nizam Shah I more than 500 years ago. This fort is different from most other forts. It is round in shape and there is a deep moat that surrounds it. Guess what? This fort is still in use. During the Indian independence struggle, the British imprisoned many Indian leaders here.
In fact, even Jawaharlal Nehru, who became India's first prime minister, was jailed here. He wrote his famous book *Discovery of India* while he was a prisoner.

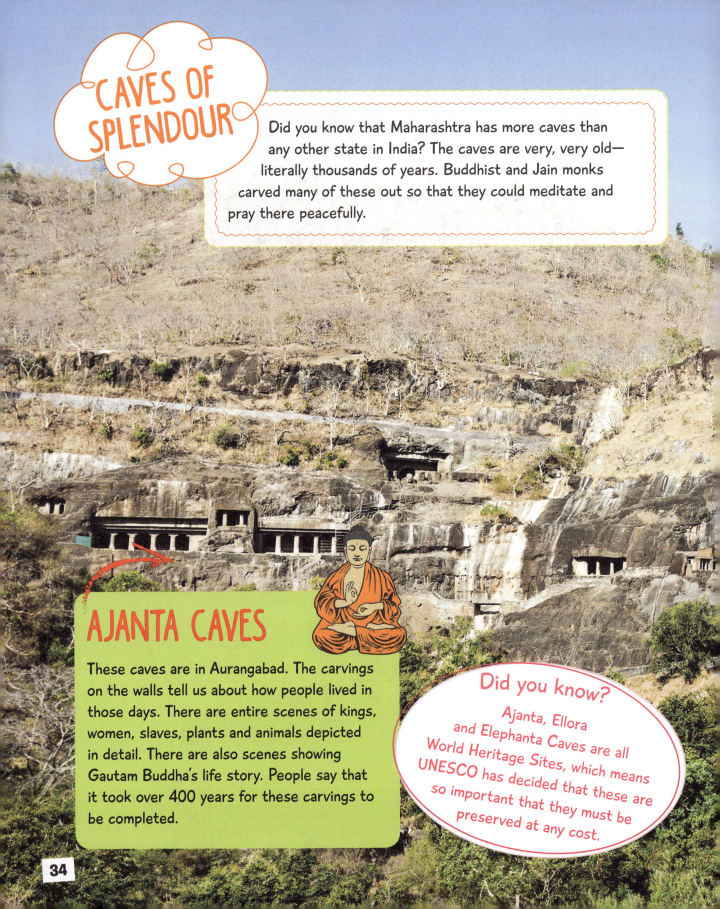

CAVES OF SPLENDOUR

Did you know that Maharashtra has more caves than any other state in India? The caves are very, very old—literally thousands of years. Buddhist and Jain monks carved many of these out so that they could meditate and pray there peacefully.

AJANTA CAVES

These caves are in Aurangabad. The carvings on the walls tell us about how people lived in those days. There are entire scenes of kings, women, slaves, plants and animals depicted in detail. There are also scenes showing Gautam Buddha's life story. People say that it took over 400 years for these carvings to be completed.

Did you know?

Ajanta, Ellora and Elephanta Caves are all World Heritage Sites, which means UNESCO has decided that these are so important that they must be preserved at any cost.

THE ELLORA CAVES

There are thirty-four amazing caves here—Hindu, Buddhist and Jain. Each of these have complicated carvings of stories or explanations of their religion. There are pillars, panels and deities all over. It just proves how people of different religions worked together in peace all those years ago.

ELEPHANTA CAVES

These beautiful caves are just a quick boat ride away from Mumbai. The most amazing here is the Shiva Temple. There are many stories about these. Some say a great warrior prince named Pulakesin II ordered these carvings to celebrate a victory. Others say that soldiers of ancient armies did their target practice in these caves, using them to keep enemies away. They say that the same craftsmen who carved the Ellora Caves also worked here.

THE SATURDAY BUILDING

That is literally what Shanivaar Vaada means. This is a wonderful palace built by the Peshwas. The story goes that they began the construction by collecting mud from the Lal Mahal nearby. The doors of the palace were so strong that no enemy could break them down.

A TURKISH CONNECTION

A tower known as Chand Minar in a place called Daulatabad was built by Sultan Ala-ud-din Bahman. He built this nearly 600 years ago to celebrate the fact that he captured a nearby fort. The design of the tower is similar to buildings in Turkey, which are decorated with blue coloured tiles from Persia. You can see a drawbridge, a cannon and studded gates that remind you of how life was in those days.

THE RED BUILDING

Lal Mahal is the place in Pune where a young Shivaji spent his childhood. If you ever go here, you will see pictures on the walls that portray amazing stories from Shivaji's life. You will also see statues of Jijamata, Shivaji's mother. This is where Shivaji cut off the fingers of Shaista Khan (who was a general in the Mughal army and was sent to kill Shivaji) when he tried to escape from a window of Lal Mahal. Oooh! This looks like an exciting place to visit.

JUMBLED UP

The names of some of these monuments are scrambled up. Can you help Pushka unscramble them?

1. A wonderful palace that makes you think of the weekends
   RAAVNIHAS AVAAD _____

2. It's red and a famous man spent his childhood there
   ALL LAHAM _____

3. This fort has a beautiful moat all around to keep enemies out
   GDAARAHEMN _____

4. This cave doesn't have a trunk so why does it have this name?
   ATANHPELE _____

A TOMB IN THE MIDDLE OF THE SEA

The Haji Ali Dargah in Mumbai is an amazing sight. It is right in the middle of the sea. It is a tomb where Haji Ali, a Muslim Saint, was buried. People from all over the world come here to pay respect. They have to cross a narrow path on the sea to reach this tomb. When it is high tide, the path is completely covered with water. So it can be reached only during low tide. How exciting!

Did you know?
Almost 15,000 people visit this tomb every day! Must be crowded.

THE GATEWAY OF INDIA

This amazing gateway is in the big, bustling city of Mumbai. It was constructed during the British era in India. It was built to welcome King George and Queen Mary to India when they visited. It is right on the seafront because this is where ships used to dock. There are steps leading down from the gateway, and even today people use these steps to enter boats and ferries.

A HOLY SPOT

Trimbakeshwar Temple is a really old temple near the city of Nashik. It is important to Hindus because it is just one of the twelve spots in India where an original Shiva 'linga' appeared by itself. People say that one of the Peshwas rebuilt this temple. It has a tank of water in the middle, which is where people believe the sacred river Godavari originated. People come from far and wide for a holy dip. Once every twelve years, the Kumbh Mela is held here.

The Kumbh Mela is one of the largest gatherings of people anywhere in the world! Imagine how crowded it must be getting.

Working hard

What do people living here do to earn money, Daadu Dolma?

Well, some of India's biggest cities are in Maharashtra. And so are some of India's largest industries. So there are many kinds of jobs people have. Let's see some of them . . .

FARMER, FARMER, WHAT DO YOU GROW?

A lot of people in Maharashtra are farmers. The Konkan region has lovely mango orchards, and the farmers there grow some of the yummiest mangoes in India. Other farmers grow grapes and oranges too! And still others grow sugar cane. Of course, they also cultivate regular crops like wheat, rice and pulses, like in other parts of India, but these fruits are special to Maharashtra.

FACTORIES AND FACTORIES

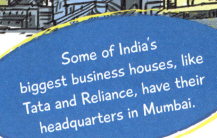

Because Bombay (now Mumbai) was such a busy port, a lot of industries were set up in Maharashtra. In fact, Maharashtra is one of the most industrialized states in India. There are factories that make chemicals, textiles, petroleum and many other things. So lots of people work either in these factories or in offices that help manage and sell what these factories produce.

Some of India's biggest business houses, like Tata and Reliance, have their headquarters in Mumbai.

MONEY MONEY MONEY

Did you know?
A stock market is just like a market. But instead of buying and selling goods, people buy and sell the shares they own in companies.

Mumbai is called the financial capital of India. That is because many big banks and other finance companies are based here. India's biggest stock market is also in Mumbai. So you can imagine how many millions of people work in financial services.

MOVIE TIME

The great big city of Mumbai is where loads and loads of Hindi movies are made. People call it Bollywood. There is a big TV industry here as well! So there are many people who work in the entertainment industry in Maharashtra—as actors, directors, designers, singers and musicians. Oh, it's a long, long list.

WEAVING MAGIC

Did you know that the weavers of Maharashtra create beautiful designs on silk? The most famous is the Paithani sari. For more than 2000 years, generations of people have been creating this amazing weave, which is made of silk and gold thread. They weave fruits, birds and flowers in the most amazing colours. Women love wearing these saris for special occasions.

CRAFTING SLIPPERS

In the region called Kolhapur, there are many people who hand-make a famous style of slipper. These are called Kolhapuri chappals. These slippers were worn by people even thousands of years ago. They are so famous that people buy them all over the world.

THE FAMOUS DABBAWALAS OF MUMBAI

The dabbawalas of Mumbai are famous all over the world. Guess what their job is? Carrying lunch boxes from people's homes to their offices, so that office goers get nice, hot lunches. Dabbawalas are famous because they have a complicated system that works like a relay race. A dabbawala picks up the dabba from someone's home. He passes it on to the next, who passes it on, and it goes on till it reaches the desk of the person it is meant for.

I sure would love to see what's inside the dabbas!

Did you know?
The delivery system of the dabbawalas is so amazing and unique that business and management students in famous universities like Harvard try and learn from it.

SAME OR Different

Look carefully at these two dabbawalas. How many differences can you spot?

43

Yum yum yum

TWO TYPES OF COOKING STYLES

Maharashtrians cook two kinds of food. One is what they cook on the long coastline that is called Konkan. It is called Konkan cuisine. The other is what people cook in the inner parts of Maharashtra. This is called Varadi cuisine.

KONKAN CUISINE

The food here is similar to what people eat in Goa—but not exactly the same. People use lots of coconut in everything. They also add tamarind in their food. Of course, since they live on the coast, they make amazing fish and crab curries too!

PITHLA BHAKRI OR ZUNKA BHAKRI

These are both very similar and equally popular dishes made of gram flour. People eat them with rotis made of jowar. Because this is an inexpensive dish, villagers make this a lot. Now it is considered a delicacy even in restaurants. People eat it with a strong and very spicy garlic chutney called thecha.

VARADI CUISINE

When people say Maharashtrian food, they often mean Varadi food. This is cooked in places like Kolhapur. It can be spicy all right! They use lots of chilli and garlic to cook this cuisine. Peanuts are also used in this style of cooking. It has many really tasty dishes.

SOFT AND SWEET

Puran poli is a yummy sweet bread that people make especially during the festival of Holi. It is made with flour that is stuffed with a sweet gram paste. People eat it soaked in milk or doused in warm ghee. Yummmm!

> Vada Pav can also be called the Indian cousin of the popular burger.

VADA PAV

The street food of Mumbai has become famous everywhere. Vada pav, which used to be a cheap food for mill workers returning home at midnight, has become a delicacy. It is a potato dumpling, squashed inside a pav (bread) and eaten with chilli and spicy chutneys.

MISAL PAV

This is another treat. It is a mix of sprouts served in a curry style and eaten with pav.

BHEL PURI

Everyone knows this amazing snack. It is puffed rice with onions, potatoes, and sweet and spicy chutneys. It is found on many street corners.

GANPATI BAPPA'S FAVOURITE

Modaks are sweet dumplings that can be steamed or fried. They are stuffed with a mixture of coconut and jaggery. People make modaks during Ganesh Chaturthi because it is considered to be Ganesha's favourite food.

AWESOME AMTI

Amti basically means curry. People in Maharashtra make lots of types of amtis that they eat with rice.

CRACK THE CODE

Crack this code and see what Pushka is trying to tell Daadu Dolma.

| I = 1 | A = 2 | Y = 3 | H = 4 | M = 5 | U = 6 |
| R = 7 | G = 8 | N = 9 |

1   2 5   4 6 9 8 7 3
__ ___ _____

What to wear?

Look how long this cloth is. What is it?

That is a dhoti. It's what men wear in villages. Come, I'll tell you more about the traditional clothes of Maharashtra.

HEADGEAR FOR MEN

There is a lot of interesting headgear that men wear, particularly in villages. They either wear a folded cotton cap or a turban. The turban is known as a pheta or pagadi.

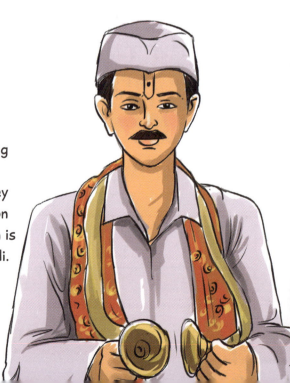

DHOTI AND SHIRT

A lot of men in villages wear a dhoti, which is a long, long cloth that is wrapped in a particular way around the waist. This is worn with either a shirt or kurta. Sometimes they wear a jacket, known as a bandi, over the shirt.

THE WHOLE NINE-YARDS

Women in Maharashtra wear saris. Traditionally, they wore really long saris, which were nine yards long. They draped it a complicated way. This is called the nauvaari sari.

Now, of course, people in cities wear modern clothes. Women and men wear jeans, shirts and T-shirts.

SPECIALLY FOR GIRLS

Young girls used to wear a long skirt with a blouse. This is called a parkar polka. Now girls wear jeans and frocks, and they wear a parkar polka only for special occasions.

Pheta fun

Pushka wants to wear a pheta. Can you draw it on his head and colour it too?

Autograph, please?

"I have my autograph book ready. Who are we going to meet, Daadu?"

"There are some really great people who are from Maharashtra. Some of them we already met when we talked about Maharashtra's amazing history. But let's meet some more."

LOKMANYA TILAK

He was a great freedom fighter during India's freedom struggle. He is the one who began the tradition of public celebrations of Ganpati.

BABA AMTE

Along with his wife, Baba Amte worked long and hard to help poor and ill people suffering from leprosy.

BABASAHEB AMBEDKAR

He was a highly educated economist. He worked all his life to uplift the 'untouchables' who were ostracized by the Indian caste system.

BAHINABAI

She was a great poet-saint who wrote spiritual poetry. She wrote about how hard it was to be a woman in her time, since life was difficult for them. She was a devotee of Lord Vithoba.

VINOBA BHAVE

He was a great believer in peace and non-violence. He worked closely with Mahatma Gandhi and set up many ashrams to help the poor. He also wrote many books through which he spread his message of peace.

MAHARSHI KARVE

He was a great man who worked all his life to empower women.

BAL THACKERAY

He was the man who started the Shiv Sena—a group that comprises followers of Shivaji Maharaj. He inspired thousands of youth to join and work with him to make a difference to the people of Maharashtra.

P.L. DESHPANDE

Known affectionately as Pula, he was a brilliant writer who wrote amazingly humourous books and plays. One of his most famous books, *Batatyachi Chaal*, is about life in a chawl.

S.L. KIRLOSKAR

He was a great businessman who built a huge empire. Even now, his children and grandchildren run the business.

BAL GANDHARVA

He was one of Maharashtra's greatest performers. He was especially famous for his performances as female characters, since in those days, women were not allowed to act.

JITENDRA ABHISHEKI

Though his family is known to be originally from Goa, he is a big name in Maharashtra and has sung many, many songs in Marathi.

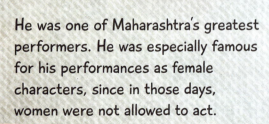

SACHIN TENDULKAR
Who doesn't know this amazing cricketer who became world number one at the prime of his career!

DR SHREERAM LAGOO
He was a terrific actor who performed in plays and movies too.

MADHURI DIXIT
She is a beautiful actress who swept the movie industry. She still acts in Hindi movies.

DADA KONDKE
He was a famous actor. The people of Maharashtra adore him for his humour.

WHAT'S ODD?

Pushka is confused. Help him figure out which name is odd in each of the rows.

BABA AMTE	VINOBA BHAVE	DADA KONDKE	BABASAHEB AMBEDKAR
MADHURI DIXIT	DADA KONDKE	SACHIN TENDULKAR	DR SHREERAM LAGOO
VINOBA BHAVE	BAHINABAI	P.L. DESHPANDE	MADHURI DIXIT

Once upon a time . . .

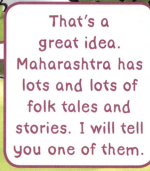

"Now, Daadu Dolma, tell us a story from Maharashtra."

"That's a great idea. Maharashtra has lots and lots of folk tales and stories. I will tell you one of them."

THE STORY OF EKKI AND DOKKI

Ekkeshi and Dokkeshi were two sisters who lived in a tiny village in Maharashtra with their parents. They were named that because Ekkeshi had only one hair growing on her little head, while Dokkeshi had two. In Marathi, 'kesh' means hair. People called them Ekki and Dokki.

Now Dokki was very proud because she had two hairs. She laughed at poor Ekki because she had only one. In fact, even their parents were nicer to Dokki and thought she looked beautiful. Ekki felt very hurt and decided to run away. And one morning, she did.

She was making her way through some fields when she suddenly heard a voice saying, 'I am so thirsty. Please give me some water.' To her surprise, it was a mehendi bush speaking. Ekki was kind. She fetched some water from a nearby stream and watered the bush. The bush brightened up at once.

Ekki walked on. She heard a voice saying, 'I am so hungry. Please give me some food.' It was a thin cow talking. Ekki was very kind. She found a big bunch of hay and fed the cow. The cow felt better at once.

Ekki walked on. She was tired and thirsty. She saw a small hut and decided to ask for water. She walked to the entrance of the hut.

An old, old woman sat there. As soon as she saw Ekki, she said, 'Come in, Ekki. I was waiting for you.' Ekki was surprised. She went into the hut. To her delight, there was a big thali with lots of food waiting for her.

'Eat,' said the old woman. 'You must be hungry.' Ekki nodded. She sat on the floor and ate everything on the thali. She was wiping her mouth, feeling very full indeed, when she felt something strange on her shoulder.

To her amazement, her hair had suddenly grown long. It was longer than her ears, longer than her cheek, longer than her shoulders. It went all the way down her back.

She clapped her hands in delight. The old woman looked on with a smile.

'You deserve this because you are a kind little girl,' she said.

Ekki thanked her. She rushed home to show her sister and parents what had happened.

When she got home, Dokki stared at her angrily. 'How did this happen,' she said, stamping her foot.

When Ekki told her, she rushed off to do the same.

But Dokki wasn't as kind as her sister Ekki had been. She ignored the mehendi bush that asked for water. She refused to feed the cow that asked to be fed. She rushed to the little hut instead.

Dokki found the old woman meditating on the bed outside the hut.

'Old woman, where is the magic food that will give me hair?' she demanded rudely. 'I must have it at once.'

The old woman ignored her. Dokki waited all day and all night. But the old woman didn't move.

Finally, the old woman opened her eyes. 'Dokki, you will not get the food because you are not kind like your sister. You can wait all you want, but you aren't going to get anything.'

Poor Dokki gave up. She went home sadly. She had learnt her lesson. From that day on, she was never nasty to Ekki—or to anyone else! As for Ekki, she continued to be kind to everyone. And they all lived together for a long, long time.

TRAVEL DIARY

Have you enjoyed this trip to Maharashtra with your friends Mishki and Pushka—and, of course, with Daadu Dolma?

Now you can make your own Maharashtra diary. And if you ever visit Maharashtra, make sure you take pictures and put them in the photo box.

The first place I would visit in Maharashtra:

_____

If I ever meet Sachin Tendulkar, this is what I would say to him:

_____

The one dish I am definitely going to eat:

_____

The monument I think is the most interesting:

_____

The one famous person from Maharashtra I would love to meet:

_____

If I were from Maharashtra, I would like to live in the city of:
_____

The festival from Maharashtra that I think is the most fun:
_____

The five words that I think describe Maharashtra the best are:
_____
_____
_____
_____
_____

My Maharashtra memories:

ANSWERS

page 9 WHAT'S ODD
Arabian Sea, Lake Michigan, Malls

page 13 CRAZY CROSSWORD

Down
1. Monsoon   4. Mango   3. Rice
6. June   9. Tapi   11. Grapes

Across
2. Bajra   5. Narmada   7. Pune
8. Cotton   10. Oranges 12. Cash
13. Tropics   14. Fertile

page 19 WORD GRID

D	E	P	S	H	I	V	A	J	I	D
B	F	E	E	F	G	R	J	V	E	A
A	F	S	A	M	B	H	A	J	I	C
J	C	H	C	W	B	W	E	F	B	D
I	C	W	V	S	D	S	S	F	H	G
R	C	A	F	Z	A	L	K	H	A	N
A	U	R	A	N	G	Z	E	B	V
O	V	B	U	E	F	X	W	V	F	E

page 21 HIDDEN WORDS

Here are some of the words you can form: den, did, die, din, dip, end, ice, inn, nip, pee, pen, pic, pie, pin, cine, deed, deep, dice, died, dine, epic, iced, need, nice, nine, pine, pence, pined, diced, dined, ended, niece, penne, piece, decide, deepen, denied, depend, indeed, needed, pended, pieced

page 23 MATCH THE WORDS
Where?—Kuthey?; Tomorrow—Udya; Day after tomorrow—Parva; Come soon—Lavkar yay; Thank you—Dhanyavad; I don't want—Mala nako

page 29 SHADOW PLAY
C

page 31 WORD LADDER
CRAWL, BAWL, BALL, ALL

page 37 JUMBLED UP
SHANIVAAR VAADA, LAL MAHAL, AHMEDNAGAR, ELEPHANTA

page 43 SAME OR DIFFERENT

page 47 CRACK THE CODE
I AM HUNGRY

page 53 WHAT'S ODD
Dada Kondke, Sachin Tendulkar, Madhuri Dixit